Everything In-between

'An incredibly accomplished writer who leads with heart and sincerity - definitely one to watch' — **Joseph Coelho**

troika

Published by TROIKA
First published 2026

Troika Books Ltd, Well House, Green Lane, Ardleigh CO7 7PD, UK
www.troikabooks.com

Collection designed and typeset by Wendy Mach, White Stone Pages

A CIP catalogue record for this book is available from the British Library

ISBN 978-1-912745-45-6
1 3 5 7 9 10 8 6 4 2

Printed in Poland at Totem.com.pl

every thing in-between

Poems by Shagufta K. Iqbal

troika

*I want to thank all five of my children, my cats,
and my husband. For the inspiration, the listening ear, and for
providing me with a place I can call home.*

To you I dedicate this book.

Contents

Introduction

Home means different things to different people.

We sometimes find ourselves in places that don't feel like a home, but we try to make it feel like one. Then sometimes magically we find ourselves somewhere that is just perfect.

Most importantly it is about who we love, and how much we can love. How home is something we carry within ourselves. How all the people and all our experiences are part of our journey towards our sense of accepting and honouring ourselves and our stories.

Everything In-between

I am fasting.
I am Fajr and Maghrib.
I am praying 5 times a day.
I am Jummah Prayers once a week.
I am Sehri and Iftar, dawn and dusk.
I am the all-you-can-eat buffet with your family.
I am daal and roti, and chicken and chips,
and fish finger sandwiches.
I am a full English Breakfast,
with the halal sausages, of course.
I am samosas and kebabs,
but with the ketchup and the mayo.

I am The Great British Bake Off.
I am Bollywood movies on a Friday night.
I am shopping malls on a Saturday afternoon,
I am pink Kashmiri tea especially.
I am the Epping Forest,
luscious dewy green,
a wet damp spring,
I am a hot Indian summer.

Everything In-between

I am all places in one body,
I am no borders,
I am Free Palestine and Kashmir.
I am Close Yarl's Wood.

I am Shagufta,
spelt S-H-A-G-U-F-T-A,

and yes, you gotta pronounce it right.
I am meh Punjabi bolniya,
And sometimes when I am feeling posh
I am indeed, and most certainly.

I am hoodies and trainers on some days.
I am shalwar kameez and hijab at the mosque.
I am almost always jhumka earrings and my Casio watch.
And I am hennah patterns on Eid day.

I am not one or the other.
It is as simple as can be,
I am me.
Nothing more, nothing less.
Easy peasy, lemon squeezy,
nothing in-betweeny
I am simply ME.

This City

Isn't it just so pretty –
this city, this city?
I said, 'Isn't it just so pretty?
This city, this city.'

All the people it holds,
The stories it's told,
This city has a heart of gold,
Its magic never gets old.

Isn't it just so pretty –
this city, this city?
I said, 'Isn't it just so pretty?
This city, this city.'

This city is as grey as rain.
This city offers warm hubs.
Has the busy track of train,
and its many football clubs.

Everything In-between

Isn't it just so pretty –
this city, this city?
I said, 'Isn't it just so pretty?
This city, this city.'

This city is market stalls,
and Carnaby St lights,
ancient tower walls,
museums and tourist sights.

Isn't it just so pretty –
this city, this city?
I said, 'Isn't it just so pretty?
This city, this city.'

This city is its famous river,
and the Underground,
sirens that make you quiver,
and carnival sounds.

Isn't it just so pretty –
this city, this city?
I said, 'Isn't it just so pretty?
This city, this city.'

Sometimes this city has bad days.
Sometimes it chews us up,
this city moves in mad ways,
and sometimes we feel we're not enough.

Then I remind myself, that most of all,
this city is you, and you and you and you.
And every single soul
trying hard to make it through,
playing their bit
keeping this city alive,
the whole of it.

Isn't it just so pretty –
this city, this city?
I said, 'Isn't it just so pretty?
This city, this city.'

Immerse Yourself in The Red City

It is made up of a bustling night market,
full of colours, tinges of pinks and reds.
With glittering lights, majestic cobras and
musicians with velvet hats on their heads.

The tinkling sounds of water fountains,
the beeping of cars, and ding of bicycle bells.
The Azaan breaking into the afternoon hubbub.
This city has so many stories and tales to tell.

Between the aroma of ras el hanout spices,
the heady fragrance of jasmine is in the air.
From the eucalyptus oils that linger in the hammam,
to the golden thick smells of argan oil for your tired hair.

The city is a feast.
It is the taste of fresh orange juice,
buttery couscous and tender slow roast lamb,
finished with orange blossom desserts, and French mousse.

This city feels like home.
Where Atlas Mountains peer in from a distance.
A haven, with hidden shady green-leafed gardens,
and a proud and rich history of colonial resistance.

Packed Lunch

Oh no! It is lunch time at school,
and I've got packed lunch again!
And no, it is not what you think!
A main, a snack and a drink!
Instead...
It's my mum's famous chicken biryani.
My friend Susan and I are in the lunch hall,
and as I discreetly open my lunchbox,
Susan leans in, sly as a fox.
'Ewwwww, what's that?' she says.
I slam close my lunchbox.
'Nothing,' I say quickly, cheeks flushed,
heart racing, palms sweaty.
I wish I was having what Susan was having:
school dinner meatballs and spaghetti.

I keep telling my mum,
I don't want her pilau rice,
Her keema and mattar,
samosa chaat,
or roti with butter.
I just want grey hummus and carrot sticks,
I want plain crackers,

dry cheese sandwiches,
I emphasise the word plain.
I complain and I complain and I complain.

Until finally...
My packed lunch feels lighter than usual...
With hopeful optimism I open the box...
And there to my absolute delight – clingfilm wrapped –
my cheese-sandwich lunch!
I show Susan and she smiles.
I take a big greedy bite...
And... Yuck!

I think mum was right...
I rummage around
looking for something delicious to be found,
something tasty and familiar.
Instead, I find a sticky note,
there like always.
Today it reads:
'Love you lots, like Jelly Tots,'
Signed off by Mum.

First published by Otter-Barry Books and Apples and Snakes in 'Spin!', 2024

First Day at My New School

I will be invisible	The school dinners will be the most delicious, most scrumptious, most wonderfully laid out feasts
The school trips will be out of this world, via rockets launched into space	The school uniform will look weird and uncomfortable on me as I walk into my new classroom
The teachers will be mean, and won't know how to pronounce my name	It will have a football pitch as big as Wembley Stadium

It will have the most exciting and elaborate drama productions ever hosted by a school	I won't make new friends; like a shadow on the wall I will be left lonely
The journey to school will be calming and soothing, weaving its way next to a glittering canal	The playground will be huge and inviting, full of giant leaf-giving trees
Everything will be new and scary, and even worse they will have Maths tests everyday	If you miss breakfast at home, there will be an abundance of bagels, a continental-style breakfast lying in wait.

The School Play

In the school play,
Sara auditioned for the role of the main character.
But Sara did not get it.
Instead, she was the understudy.
Even though she had learnt all the lines,
knew all the actions,
practised all the jokes down to a T,
perfected the audience interactions.
But Sara was just the understudy,
and not the leading lady.
Not like Alice, who was the lead role.

So, the night before the big show,
Sara prayed.
Sara prayed Alice got sick.
That Alice lost her voice.
(Not forever, but at least until the final show.)
Was blown away by a freak gust of wind.
Had a poisonous reaction to her breakfast.
Caught a rare and exotic cough.
Got lost in one of the many aisles in the local supermarket.
Choked on an 'It's too spicy' samosa.
Was torn in two by her terrible toddler brother.

Was swallowed by the washing machine.
Combusted in her bed while rehearsing her lines.
Sara prayed.

But on the morning of the school play,
Alice turned up in costume, bright and healthy.
And Sara had to admit she was relieved.

That morning, Sara was the best understudy she could be.
She was supportive and helpful.
Sara was full of genuine encouragement.
And she hoped, one day when *she* was the leading lady,
she would have an understudy as excellent as she was.

SPORTS DAY

Today should be renamed the WORST DAY,
not the whole school summer SPORTS DAY!
Ms Begum keeps blowing her loud whistle.
Bobby is the corner having a cry.
Mr Crookshank keeps shouting:
Do your best, and make sure you try!
Mr Jones has misplaced the runner-up certificate,
Gurpreet has failed to show up,
and Sophie has just thrown up!
Leon is showing off his 600-metre win.
Andre is having a tantrum because he didn't come first,
and Leonie's javelin throw has landed in the bin!
Today really is just the worst.
Li is teaching everyone how to do cartwheels.
Rita has crossed her arms and sat down in the middle of the relay.
Haider has joined her protest for *Anti-Sports Day*!
Mohammed's baby sister has pulled all the trophies off the display,
And Mr Crookshank has sat on the eggs for the egg-and-spoon race!
Jordan has fallen flat on his face!
And the Headteacher makes an announcement:
Can everyone please make sure you've tied your laces,

before you embark on any races!
What can I say,
today really is the worst day.
The parents are cheering so much some have lost their voices.
Sophie's nanny has pins and needles in her hands from clapping so much.
Toby has run so fast he can't seem to stop –
he's halfway out the school gates!
Sports Day is a total flop!
Daniel's dog, Monty, has interrupted the hurdles!
Daniel's dad is chasing Monty across the field!
Everyone cheers and agrees Monty should win a trophy!
The sun is shining its bright hot rays,
while we are all sweltering.
And then finally,
after a long hard day,
we hear the delicious sounds
of the ice-cream van!

Shoe Laces

How am I supposed to tie my laces?
I keep tripping in playground races,
because they keep coming undone!

Hassan says
It's simple, you do it like this:
You cross the helicopter blades
You loop the loop
You hoop the hoop
Then swoop the swoop
and boom
laces are done!

But he's lost me at hoop the hoop!
I look at my shoes—
they look like hissing snakes.

Sharifa says
It's simple, you do it like this:
You make the bunny ears,
You twist the twist,
Then twirl the twirl,
then whirl the whirl

And boom
Laces are done!

But she's lost me at twirl the twirl!
I look at my shoes—
it's like grappling with octopus arms!

Adam says
It's simple, you do it like this:
You make the bow for the present,
You pinny it down,
Then jimmy it along,
Then shimmy it through,
and boom
laces are done!

It is Monday morning, and I head downstairs,
ready to grapple frustratingly with my laces.
But instead, I see a pair of shiny new shoes,
with a strong Velcro strap across the top.
Dad winks, and we race out the door,
with nothing to slow me down today!

Dear Bully

I know I cannot say this to your face.
You would laugh,
or worse yet hit me,
for daring to speak out against you.
And I know I would cry hot lava tears,
in the girls' toilets on my own,
so no one would know how much your words sear.
But if I could erupt my feelings into the classroom,
full of classmates watching me being shamed once again,
I would say this:

Yes, I am fuming.
My anger grows smoke,
like a dark cloud.
On the days you smirk, and spit and laugh,
deep down I am an ash of rage in quiet response.
My fists curl up,
my knuckles igneous rock.
I wish I could stop the words that your mouth spews out.
Instead, I stand tall, hold my head high,
I take the hit.
The ground under me opens like a crater,
my cheeks turn fire red.

Your words may cut,
but I stand here still,
stare you back in the face.
And wonder what embers burn inside,
that make you smirk, and spit and laugh.
Even though I try to take the advice of grown-ups,
of, 'Oh, just ignore her.'

Dear Bully, this molten lava of yours
may catch you on fire.
But quietly, silently,
I will stand here still.

First published by Otter-Barry Books and Apples and Snakes in 'Spin!', 2024

Bath

My old stomping ground is this shapeshifting city.
Changing every time I visit its cobbled streets.
This city is quietly trying to escape his history,
the legacy of plantations, sugar, and blood.
He re-invents himself like a Vogue icon.
Through windows in sandstone homes,
he invites me with bright smiling eyes.
The botanical gardens and crescents
crown the head of this gentle giant.
His mouth is made up of farmers' markets,
with rows of cheeses, pickles, pies, and jams.
I get pulled in by his classic charm and wit.
His laughter is a Children's Literature Festival,
full of mystery and stories that captivate us.
His arms are canals and riverbeds,
open palmed for exploring boats and punting.
His stomach is the ancient waters of the Roman Baths.
I want to forgive this beautiful time-capsule friend of mine,
munch on scones and buns with clotted cream,
take in the beauty of his carved cathedrals.
But I wish he would be more honest with me,
own his mistakes like a true friend would,
try his hardest to make amends.

So, I hold out an olive branch to him,
and wait for him to receive it with some modesty.

Here or There

Sometimes I live with my mum,
and sometimes I live with my dad.
Sometimes I get confused,
and then I get really mad!

I don't know if I am there, or if I am here.
Am I near?
Or I am far?

Sometimes I live with my mum,
and sometimes I live with my dad.
I find I am always missing someone.
It makes me so sad.

But then, I remember,
I have two homes.
One with my favourite shalwar kameez,
and one where we keep honey bees!
One bedroom with my favourite reading nook,
one with my favourite blanket and book.
I have two gardens!
One with my pet tortoise!
And one with my football goal post!

And I get two birthday parties a year,
and that is quite unusual I hear.
And to top it off,
I also get two Eid presents!
But most of all, I have two parents.
Both who love me very much.

And that is something truly special,
and it makes me feel loved, whether I am here, there or anywhere.

New House Noises

Ssssh! Can you hear it?
A gurgling swirl monster is in the toilet—
he is especially loud at nighttime!

Ssssh! Can you hear it?
A long-fingered monster taps the window—
she is especially loud at nighttime!

Ssssh! Can you hear it?
A heaving creaky monster is in the attic—
he is especially loud at nighttime!

Ssssh! Can you hear it?
A humming munch monster is in the kitchen—
she is especially loud at nighttime!

Ssssh! Can you hear it?
A howling shadow monster is on the walls—
he is especially loud at nighttime!

Ssssh! Can you hear it?
Morning birdsong that has scared the monsters away.
I have survived my first night in our new home!

The Little Humble Bee

They say the forests are on fire,
and I don't think recycling milk bottles will save them.
I am just one little person—
What difference can I make?

There are cities flooding, waters swallowing them whole,
and I don't think buying fewer clothes will save them.
I am just one little person—
What difference can I make?

There are icebergs melting into the rising oceans,
and I don't think walking to school is going to save them.
I am just one little person—
What difference can I make?

But then I see the humble bumble bee.
She is just one little bee,
but my goodness what a difference she makes.

Little Bellies

Miss Khan tells us about the sable shearwater,
with its long brown wings, with streaked white tips.
'This bird is from the shores of a crescent-shaped island.'
Miss Khan stands at the front of the class,
a gentle and firm fount of knowledge.
Sometimes, it is hard to hear Miss Khan
over the rumbling of our morning hunger.
Miss Khan, without making a fuss,
places small plates in our light-filled classroom,
where we help ourselves to jam-slathered bagels.

'The birds are so full of dangerous plastic,
that their bellies make crunch and crash noises.'
She shows us images of bright plastic throwaways,
bottle caps, cutlery, and unidentifiable pointed shards.
We make classroom art, and imagine how to repurpose
bottle top lids into colourful mosaics for our walls.

While at the back of our class lie pink jammy O's,
like a little flock of round laughing bellies.

Summer Holidays

In summer we did not ski in the Alps,
We did not summer in the South of France,
We did not visit music festivals in tents.
Instead, we picnicked through our summer holidays.
Whole families gathered on a patch of grass,
between the M32, and an ochre-coloured river.
Plastic roll-up mats, unravelled onto the ground.
Tupperware revealed mountains of samosas,
platters of kebabs, and heaped valleys of delicious rice.
The mothers set about laying frugal feasts,
only to be chased away by an unleashed dog.
And there was always the one auntie,
who knew how to make a masala pasta
that the kids could not get enough of.
Melons would be split open like the crescent moon.
Orange segments divided between
the bestest of friends.
Bottles of fizzy drinks and Rooh Afza,
the plonk of ice cubes filling the air.
A generous selection of sweets for the kids,
where a new discovery would be made
about a favourite sweet containing gelatine!
Another one to cross off the list.

Around the picnic we would hopscotch and weave footballs,
until we were ushered away.

We would take it in turns to push one another on the swings
Balance as many bodies as possible on the see-saw

We played Stuck-In-The-Mud, Bulldog, and 44 Release All,

until someone with a belly full of sweets and fizzy drink,
threw up on the roundabout ride,

and we would run from a playground full of cooties.

In our Matchstick trainers,
neon T-shirts bought from the Fruit Market,
dark curly hair, and missing baby teeth,
with no money from the tooth fairy,

the Mothers created a world for us,
where we would feast like kings,
and listen to stories about the djinn.
Next to a deteriorating playground,
under the hum of a busy motorway,
the rare glare of the summer sun.
Their dupattas fluttering a multitude of colours,
anyone would think these magicians could transport us to

another world.

One where the tip of the Himalayas could offer itself as a
salt seasoning to our summer holiday feast.

First published by Otter-Barry Books and Apples and Snakes in 'Spin!', 2024

Missing You

My grandma would listen to music from far away.
These songs sounded strange to me.
A distant language floating in our home.
The guttural vowels.
The sharp high-pitched sounds.
The pulsating drums.
These songs made her eyes moist.
Or sometimes she would jump to her feet,
dance in circles,
clapping her hands,
a bright snap of sound.
Her bangles jingling,
her eyes sparkling,
as she would sing strange words to me.

My grandma is not here with me,
and when I miss her real bad,
I put the old cassette in the dusty HiFi.
It crackles into a slow start,
sliding back the lonely months.
And I imagine she is here,
dancing with me in the living room,
bangles jingling,

her feet pounding the worn carpet,

her hands a soft explosion into the air.

Singing words that are vaguely familiar to me:

Kitnah sonah

tainu rab neh banaya

Dil kar dekh ta rahoun

Far Away Family

My sleepy bedtimes are your hearty breakfasts.
Online games twine us together,
I click buttons on this side of the planet,
and they unfurl colours onto your screen.
Our days are filled with lots of video calls.
Gone are the days of a wired crackling voice,
Instead your faces light up our living room,
bright and clear.
On birthdays and festivals,
we send each other presents in the post.
Count down the days until they are received,
bow ties unpicked across continents.
We don't always understand each other,
I lose my words, and
you rope together different meanings.

But what I love the most is when we meet
in the summer holidays,
and play football in the park.
Unfold goals into nets,
and share our different footie tricks.
Then at the end of the day we watch stars,
and reach out for one another,
arms over each other's shoulders,
as though we had never been apart.

The Unwanted Sisters

I never needed friends.

I didn't need them at school.

I didn't need them at netball club.

I didn't need them at days on the beach.

This is because I had my many sisters.

I had a sister that I could make and build with.

I had a sister that I could share all my books with.

I had a sister I could act scenes of our favourite movies with.

I had a sister for sharing shoes and clothes, and plaiting hair with.

I never needed friends,

as I had many sisters

I was not supposed to have.

Each time a new one came along,

small and soft fisted, all yawn mouthed,

everyone was disappointed she wasn't a boy.

So, I kept adding them to my gang of unwanted sisters.

Where we would play, and pretend, and we would dream,

we would fight, we would yell, but most of all we were a team.

I never needed friends,
because I had my many sisters.
We had a secret coded language,
We understood each other without speaking.
Our problems— we shared them and we halved them.
We were a gang when a fight came knocking on our door.
Or those days when our empty stomachs grumbled and growled.
We were there for each other when the nights were loud and dark.
Or when the adults in our world were distant shadows on cold walls.

I never needed friends,
as I had my many sisters.
We grew through childhood,
knowing each other's likes and dislikes.
Sometimes we would be cruel and unkind,
knew how to press into a fragile open wound.
We would split paths and grow in different ways,
but somehow, some way, almost always, inevitably,
we would come back to each other, all roots of the same tree.

Everything In-between

I have always needed my sisters.
Around a table at the break of dawn,
Outside, birds singing Fajr prayers.
Cups full of warm milk in our hands,
suhur breakfasts in our happy bellies.
Laughter running down our faces,
our cheeks aching with wild stories,
of how we grew from girls unwanted
to the sisters we have always needed.

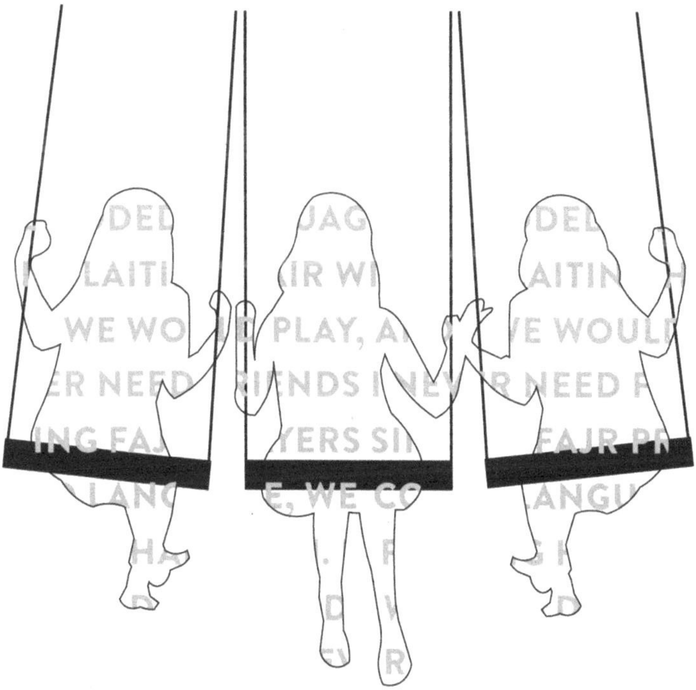

First published by Otter-Barry Books and Apples and Snakes in 'Spin!', 2024

Mirpur, Pakistan

M ountainous ranges, with snowy tips that reach up and tickle the midday sun

I rrigated fields of rice, lentils and mustard, a vast golden stretch to the horizon point

R ickshaws, motorbikes, cars and cattle weave and dodge through the city's pathways

P oems and legends rest at Khari Sharif, a shrine of marble floors and green domes

U biquitous bodies of water, in rivers and lakes, gathering with foam at the Mangla Dam

R ecognised the world over, as 'Little England', where teas and cakes are served under the watch of the Himalayas.

A place where my grandparents were born,
and where they were eventually buried.
A place that has a pull on me,
and makes itself known as a
home.

Mixing It Up

I like to mix my ketchup with my mayo
I like to mix mango with chilli
I like pineapple on my pizza
I like sweet and sour chicken
I like to mix it up a bit!
I like it upside down and left to right

I like coffee in my hot chocolate
I like ice cream with hot gulab jamum
I like coconut flavours in my spicy curry
I like apricots in my tangy tagine
I like to mix it up a bit!
I like it upside down and left to right

I like to mix my lemonade with blackberry squash
I like punchy pumpkin spice in my latte
I like beetroot in my chocolate cake
I like chocolate melted on my mint leaves
Yes, I said I like to mix it up a bit!
I like it upside down and left to right

Spice Level Championships

Contenders! Are you ready?
Weighing in at 15 grams, is the Scotch Bonnet,
flying in from the Caribbean,
with a hammer-hitting strong punch on your jerk chicken.

Scotch Bonnet is up against the Naga Nightmare
to give you the night sweats,
and who also goes by the name of the
Ghost Pepper, the Bhut Jolokia,
a favourite heavyweight champion.

Then all the way from Mexico,
we have the Jalapeño,
with a rigorous training regime
of pizza toppings and fajitas wraps,
packing a punch in your burrito.

Followed by the Carolina Reaper,
small flakes can turn a regular sauce into a lava streak.

Let's not forget the most deadly, the most memorable,
Trinidad Moruga Scorpion

Second-hottest chilli in the world
sting you for life.

Water is not enough.
Milk is not gonna cut it.
Fizzy drink has melted my taste buds.
I hold my tongue against ice cream,
But it is still on fire.
My eyes are watering.

My face is as red as a chilli pepper.
Rashes are breaking out over my face.
I don't think I will ever eat a chilli ever again!

5,

4,

3,

2,

1

and I'm out

KO!

My Brother, the Pee Monster

My brother says: *Yuck!*
He does not want to wear nappies any more.
No, no, no, he shouts.

Now I say *Yuck*
Because my brother has become the pee monster.
He's peed on the kitchen floors,
He's peed next to the cat litter box,
Even the cat said *Yuck*
He's peed when I gave him a hug,
He said I squeezed far too much.
He's peed while looking at goldfish in the pet shop,
He said the wavy water made his tummy feel funny.
He's even peed in the car seat on the way to the park.
We all had to turn around and head back home.
He's peed while having a nap,
He's even peed on Granny's lap!
He's peed in Grandpa's garden,
Right next to the rose bush and lavender shrubs.

But Mum just says, *Don't be so mean,*

We are sitting in the living room. Mum in the armchair,

me in my favourite place, the sunny spot, on the sofa.

Mum continues, *Be nice.*

I have many stories

from when you were potty training.

You should know it takes time.

Remember when you peed,

Right there, on the sofa,

in the sunny spot?

Class 5T, Period 3

Kwan says...
she likes my hair because it's wavy
I love hair her cos it's super straight.

Sita has a bob, doesn't want her hair to grow,
While Nathaniel is growing out his awesome afro.

Phoenix has a magnificent mohawk
Tammy's hair is gloriously ginger.

Amir's hair is a midnight-sky black
While Bethany has dyed her ends pink.

Serena has shaved it all off,
And asks, 'What do you all think?'

Devante has a fantastic fade,
And Surinder wears a perfect plait.

Ina's hair is cute and curly,
And Ashante has brilliant braids.

Max's hair is floppy – it falls over his eyes –
While Abdi's hair is stylishly short.

Rajpal wears his hair in a terrific topknot
And Gisele keeps her hair nice and natural.

Curtis has cool cornrows,
Mahdiya's hair is luscious and long.

Chloe's hair is bright and blonde,
And Yasmin's hair is beautiful and brown.

Miss Akhtar says...
'Yes, yes, we all have beautiful hair'
(Miss Akhtar wears hers in a bun.)
'But can we please open our books,
and turn to page twenty-one.

Let's examine propaganda in history.
How differences were not celebrated,
but used to isolate and cause misery.

Not at all like my wonderful class of 5T
who show kindness and respect.
A shining example of how the world should be.'

The Zoomies

In the middle of a snoring, snoozing, wheezing night,
my cats run around giving everyone a fright!
They flip, they zip, they whizz!
Jiving and jumping off kitchen counters,
They are somersaulting and super sonic –
Furiously flashing through the catflap,
Clawing and catapulting across the carpets,
Boldly bungee jumping down the stairs,
Careening and cartwheeling on the dining table,
Speed-of-lightning their way through the hallway.
Acrobatics avengers tumbling over trinkets and vases.

And when I greet them in the morning,
wondering about all the nighttime commotion,
they purr soft and gentle, yawn their little yawns.

Secret ninjas in the night.

The Prince Who Would Be King

The Prince is often stopped when he's out walking.
The streets are sometimes difficult to navigate,
full of hate, shadows lurk with stalkings.
The path is laid down with traps,
even with school uniform and backpacks,
sneakers and sports caps.
The Kingdom will try to accost him,
pull him aside.
Try to knock down his pride, stumble his stride,
nowhere to run and hide.
Mistake him for someone who fits the description...
The Prince wants to live like an everyday kid.
Play footie with his friends,
run around in a park,
not worry about the dark,
not hurry through the streets,
suspicious of who he meets.
Just score goals and nutmeg his mates,
then top up with a fizzy pop at the local shop,
not be forced to stop,
because he fits a description...
He wants peace, and no aggravation.

He wants to visit the new chicken-wing place,
order menu-option three.
As spicy as can be.
Walk in the sunshine, catching up with his mates.
Sharing tips and tricks for the latest games.

But the Prince keeps getting mistaken for someone who
fits the description...

The Prince wonders about this *description*
and why is it that he always seems to fit it?
Lined up in a queue
he's singled out.
Walking down the street
he's hit with it.
On a protest march
and he's gotta sit it out.
Getting ready for the plane
and he's gonna have to miss it.

The Prince twigs he's not the only one –
Kings before him
have been up against this *description*.
In a youth-group session
he learns a valuable lesson.

So on a card he writes
about his rights.
Arms himself with knowledge, with truth.
The Prince writes his *own* description.
His rules to live by –
his manifesto.

Where everyone is safe
                    to go for a stroll
                                without fitting a description.

Who Am I?

On facing myself I present a loop of eternity.
Polished and full of light, I start your day.
Getting you ready for a new school term.
I am a portal, helping you find your way.

We make silly faces and have so much fun.
Only when you are not being critical, but feel OK.
We mimic each other and do a double take.
I hold myself quietly, on the walls where I stay.

I gossip *who is the fairest of them all.*
I swallowed curious Alice, they say.
I highlight the vampire's deception.
I am a water surface on a reflective ray.

Yes, I am that whimsical dual two-faced cliché,
I do everything in reverse; it's how I like to play.
But I warn you, do not break the illusion of me,
or with seven years' bad luck I will make you pay.

Answer: *Mirror*

Belonging

Belonging is laughter.
It is a place that speaks truths,
and still feels welcoming.
It sounds like celebrations, birdsong, the Azaan,
and being surrounded by your friends.
Home is the family picnic in the garden,
The smell of a freshly baked cake.
Washing drying on the clothesline.
Our lazy day family takeaways.
The smell of pages in a new book,
coffee, lavender, and teenage sisters.
It is mint and jasmin growing in the garden.

The wind against my face,
tears in my eyes from the cold.
A happiness bundled on the sofa.
The flicker of movie night with caramel popcorn.
My cheeks hurting from laughter.
The cosiness of my bedsheets,
my cat curled in my lap,
soft fur against my fingertips.

Belonging is feeling safe,
And knowing you are accepted
for exactly who you are.

Abertawe

Take a cascading pouring of golden sand,
A dollop of purple sunsets across the skies.

Heap spoonfuls of joyous windy valleys.
rolling hills, and rocky crags of Three Cliffs Bay.

Knead in the majesty of mountains,
their snowy peaks in the far distance.

Fold in the winding cathedral-like caves,
the views from Black Mountain quarries.

Add the essence of the Welsh language,
many drops of their myths and legends.

Add a pinch of Gower's dunes, to sink toes into.
Roll in the clouds that bring seafront showers.

Simmer with the bright blues of Brombil Reservoir,
the river Tawe, and the rockpools of Penllergaer Waterfall.

Season with the tidal inlet of Paleolithic Paviland,
a limestone burial chamber facing the slow tide out at sea.

Dust with glass-roofed markets of sugared Welsh cakes,
and leave to rest the historic fortresses of Swansea castle.

Sprinkle with sailing boats over glimmering waters.
Drizzle with the fiery breath of red-scaled dragons.

Now serve me this city, a once Copperopolis,
with its rhythmic lilt, its dreamy promises of
beaches that stretch as far as the eye can see.

The Caretakers

The universe was becoming dark and void.
The stars were beginning to burn out,
like candles melting, spineless
into a puddle of tarmac.

Earth was a marble
gifted to me by my grandmother.
A small spark of light.
It was no ordinary marble.
This marble was the earth itself,
and I was a giant holding on to it.
A bubble full of breath,
in a spiralling soundless galaxy.
She held it in her palm,
open and flat.

Earth was a marble and I was a giant holding it,
every time I turn in my sleep,
the world is spinning upside down,
the stars are tumbling into a new formation.

Everything In-between

Earth was a marble full of light,
and I am the caretaker,
of its oceans, and rainforests,
its mountains, and skies.
Keeping it safe,
ready to hand over
to a small pair of hands.

Earth is a marble full of hope.
A gift to be handed with love
to my daughter,
from my grandmother.
A legacy of how we take care
of the things we love.

My Prayer Mat

Soft and velvety,
green and golden.
A gift from my favourite auntie.
A place where I share my thoughts,
and leave all my anxieties.
Five times a day,
to the sound of the Azaan,
I can switch the world off.

When I bow down to pray,
the carpet is welcoming to my fingertips.
I breathe in the essential oils on its textured threads.
I recite my prayers, and slow my breathing.
Time suddenly slows

right d o w n f o r m e .

Rainy Days

I
like
it
when it
rains. Raindrops
pitter patter on the
window pane. My family
call the sound a rim jhim
rim jhim. We watch the sharp
drops fall into our world, the rain
smoosh down on tree leaves, gather
in big puddles in the garden, fill the bird
bath generously, call rainbows into being.
We all put our raincoats on and run outside.
Dance in the rain. Kick up the puddles. And
then come back in for a long hot bath. A
bedtime story. A cosy warm drink in my
hand. Long fluffy socks snuggled up to
my knees. Rainy days can be full of
adventure and fun.

Secrets

Tarifa has shared a secret with me.
We were drawing self-portraits with charcoal,
in art class last week Monday,
when she leaned over and whispered to me.
She told me her secret quiet and afraid,
and made me promise not to tell anyone.

I know, I am her best friend,
and I made her a promise.
But Tarifa's secret is heavy.
It drains all the colour from our lives.
She carries it around wherever she goes,
it hangs on her shoulders weighing her down.
It keeps me up at night,
and makes her tired in class.
It is a shadow overcasting our lives.
It manifests in dark circles around her eyes.

Tarifa's secret makes me worry for her,
and I can see it is making her feel bad.
The secret I am holding is wanting to burst,
like watercolour bleeding out over a canvas.

Tarifa's secret is making her ill with worry.
If she fell, I would put a plaster on her cut.
If she made a mistake, I would quietly erase it.
And if she cried, I would give her a hug.
But I do not know how to help Tarifa with this secret.
Especially on days when she doesn't come into school.

Then on Thursday during school assembly
Mrs Smith tells us she is the safeguarding lead:
Please speak to me for whatever you may need
A problem shared is a problem halved
We'll try our best to make things better.

I feel bad for what I am about to do.
But where Tarifa is, I don't have a clue.
I think I can't be a very good best friend,
because I need to share Tarifa's secret,
as I can no longer hold it on my own.

But Mrs Smith says it's OK,
That I have done the right thing.
That I'm a most caring best friend, and
that some secrets should never be secrets.

After what seems like a long time,
Tarifa finally returns to school.
She seems unsure and shy,
but she's no longer tired and scared.
I'm worried she'll no longer be my friend,
but she comes rushing up and gives me a big hug.

Tarifa no longer has secrets to keep.
No heaviness that wears her down.
She is an artist's palette, full of potential.
She and Mrs Smith have a new friendship too.
They have a special room where they speak and share.

Today we draw self-portraits in art class,
Today we use bright pastel colours and endless glitter.

The Bristol Questionnaire

Please tick all that apply

My City:

- ☐ Full of bright and vivid graffiti
- ☐ A legacy of slave ships and greed
- ☐ A cacophony of carnivals and festivals

My Caer Odor*:

- ☐ The city of the gap
- ☐ A meeting place by the bridge
- ☐ The pronunciation of the terminal 'L', that I can never seem to shake

My City:

- ☐ An open mouth of an estuary
- ☐ A swashbuckling tale of pirates
- ☐ A boisterous seagull-hangout spot

My Brycg Stowe**:

- ☐ Factory fumes that called to the colonies
- ☐ The place my grandparents settled and raised their children
- ☐ The roar of flames in an Aardman hot-air balloon

My City

- ☐ More Cimon and Pero than the greed of Colston
- ☐ More 'City of Sanctuary' than hostility
- ☐ More 'Seven saints of St Pauls' than any form of bigotry

My Brigstow:

- ☐ Has the shortest motorway in England
- ☐ Is the inspiring strength of a bus boycott
- ☐ A music making, drum-and-bass banging innovator

My City:

- ☐ An architectural feat of the Floating Harbour and supersonic jets
- ☐ A feast for the eyes in rows of bright-coloured buildings
- ☐ A wildlife-film hub to the A&E corridors of *Casualty*.

My Abona***:

- ☐ Is its Iron Age hill forts and farmsteads
- ☐ Is the suspension bridge spanning across a gorge
- ☐ Is the rising of a phoenix after the Blitz

My City:

☐ Is the resting place for the Father of The Indian Renaissance

☐ A city built on blood, disguised as sugar and cocoa

☐ A city that topples injustice in the face of it

My Bristol:

☐ Makes me sad and ashamed

☐ Makes me proud and hopeful

☐ Makes itself known to me as home

** The old Welsh name for Bristol meaning 'Fort of the chasm'*

*** This is the Saxon name for Bristol meaning 'Place by the bridge'*

**** This is the Roman name for a settlement in Bristol*

What Am I?

I pull at the oceans of your imagination,
You howl and bleed at the memory of me.

You have spent centuries singing songs about me.
Your heart has wished little wishes at the sight of me.

I glow and shine when you need me most.
I run the monsters from their shadows at night.

I am a murmur, a crater, a glimmer of a dream.
A gibbous, a waning, a delicious night-sky croissant.

During Ramadan you watch out for my shapeshifting sighting,
when my arrivals are marked with festivals and celebrations.

Answer: The Moon

In My House

We have couscous and biryanis
Gnawa music and qawwali ghazals
Fruity Tagines and butter chicken
Bright kaftans and shimmering sherwanis
Nutty baklawa and glistening gulab jamuns
The Atlas Mountains and the snowy Himalayas
Trips to the sea and trips to the lakes
Red flags with stars and green ones with crescent moons
Velvety fez hats and woolly pakuls
We have Arabic and Punjabi proverbs and jokes

We are two continents in one home
Two peoples in one family
Two cultures swapping and sharing stories
Two families blended into one, making new memories.

How We Celebrate Eid

We always start by keeping watch for the new moon,
its pointed ambiguous face, the first sign of celebration,
Which is followed with henna patterns on our hands.
The red dye grows deep on my palms as I sleep carefree.
I awake to the call of the Azaan, the communal Eid prayer,
where row upon row, we kneel in leafy parks and mosques.
Then finally I am rewarded with my first brunch in a month.
Sweet semolina, milky vermicelli, pistachio-sprinkled delights.
Crumbly hashra, and rghaif pancakes with chocolate spread.

We all sit around the breakfast table in the bright daylight.
Grateful that we have been blessed to have such feasts,
while always remembering we have brothers and sisters
right across the surface of this globe who need our help,
who we cannot forget throughout the rest of the year.
Our feasts and blessings we share with Zakat donations.
Because their celebrations are our celebrations,

their joy is our joy.

And their Eid is our Eid.

THE CALL OF THE AZAAN,
THE NEW MOON
ON OUR

My Birthday

This is my first birthday without my cuzzy.
We usually plan and celebrate together.
She would mood board a theme,
and I would be a total drama queen.
She would try to blow my birthday candles out,
and I would try to smear birthday cake on her nose.
Our birthdays were our favourite time of the year.

We planned to celebrate our birthdays together
for many many more years.
Until we had poppable false teeth!
And bright white hair!
We'd say, *'Sorry, what did you say, my dear?'*

But this year my cuzzy is not here.
I do not feel like celebrating at all.
I look through our photos and silly selfies,
and cannot believe she is not on this earth.

Sometimes I hear her speaking to me still,
laughing and teasing, so loud and clear.
On days where I want to curl up in my bed,
and hide away from a world
that has lost all its fun and joy,
I imagine her dragging me out of my bed.

Let's mood board how we move forward,
she would say.
I know she would want me to have fun still,
would want the memory of birthdays to go on.

Even though I miss her,
I know she is happy where she is.
Very likely blowing out candles on clouds for me,
making wishes, and trying to lick birthday cake
off the tip of her nose with her tongue!

Inna Lillahi wa inna ilayhi raji'un.

Extraordinary Is

This world, with its aurora borealis,
the sky a musical showcase dancing over us.
Its bioluminescent shores, phytoplankton and
algae bloom sea-sparkle against crystalline beaches.

This world, with its synchronous fireflies,
bright spotlit forests bathed in a yellow hush.
Its murmurations of birdflight, the synchronised starlings.
Each bird folding itself into the centre of this hovering cloud.

This world, with its Venus flytrap,
a pink-mouthed snap, in wait of prey.
Its saltwater oysters, a journey of sand
that bloom lustrous layers of pink and white nacre.

This world, with its Arctic extremes,
tundras scattered with glaciers and permafrost.
Its pleated Sahara desert, a teasing of sand dunes with
mirages of lush oases, and spring waters lined with date trees.

Extraordinary is this world, which we have been gifted.
Extraordinary is how quickly we are damaging it.
But more extraordinary is how much power we have to fix it.

Everything In-between

Reasons to Celebrate Nablus

1. The raging beauty of an olive-tree lined Jabal al Nar
2. A living breathing history of fired mosaic tiles
3. Thick walls of ancient ruins, and people of many cultures
4. The engraved columns of the Sebastia Amphitheatre
5. Dabke dance, defiant and joyous between the strangle of check points
6. The stretchy cheesy delight of the syrupy sweet kunaffe
7. Against curfews, the moonlit cobbled streets of the Old City
8. The bubble soap aroma of the famous olive soap factories
9. The hubbub of shops and yellow taxis buzzing around Martyrs Square
10. And the serene mosques, their noble minarets that stand tall against time
11. A city full of rich life, a testament to courage and hope.
12. A land where visitors are always welcomed, and treated with cardamon coffees
13. A land populated with people, a people who are the body of the land itself

Unknown by Light

Collapsed and flooded, the Belize Blue Hole is a limestone cave of glacial memory

Memories of the turquoises of Lake Baikal, the world's oldest and deepest fresh water

Waters that are foreign to the hyper-saline Antarctica's iron-rich Blood Falls

Falling apart, like the sea between Jindo and Modo disappears, revealing a path for travellers

Travelling by boat to the bioluminescent glow worms of Waitomo Caves

Caved in like craters of the inverted Darvaza Crater which burns with wishes

Wishing on fire rainbows, as light passes through hexagonal ice crystallised

Crystal clear is the view to Iceberg Alley, where icebergs drift south, heavy and mysterious

Mystery surrounds the desert trails of sailing stones, that leave behind signs of movement

Moving through water, translucent frozen fingers of brinicles cross ocean seabeds

Seas are the underwater secret universe where even sunlight crashes and collapses.

Gerry Geranium

Dazzling green lobed leaves filled my new bedroom.
The fragrance sweet and sharp, heady and airy,
spilled from the window shelf,
where my school geranium plant sat.

Last summer, Mr Adebayo gave me the class plant.
He asked to me to take good care of it,
Make it feel like it's at home, he said.
The plant made me feel responsible and important.

During the school summer holidays
I would wake up to it every day,
turn its palmate leaves to the sun,
or spray water over its rich woody soil.

This year we moved home again.
Although mum promised it was our last move.
I would have to learn to make a new home
in a strange and unfamiliar building once again.

She held the white terse letter from the landlord,
sighed a big sigh, and her hand trembled a little.
I'm sorry, bub, I really tried. She looks tired as she apologises.
It makes me feel sad, but I don't want to make her feel worse.

So, when Mr Adebayo gave me Gerry, the class plant,
mum took a cutting, from stem to serrated leaves.
She planted it in a small bright blue plant pot,
asked me to water the hardy clustered leaves.

Gerry Jr looks for points of light whenever we move.
I watch him stretch and grow in even the smallest of places.
And I am always there to make sure he is watered and fed,
ready to spread his bright green leaves across new window frames.

The Jungle

In fields of popping pinks, greens, and blues,
the summer sun creates a bursting suntrap.
There you will find my one-person-cocooning tent,
which has snuggled me through cold nights
and damp dewy mornings.
Where I can rest after a DofE challenge,
or glitter bomb my face at festivals,
or play UNO® on a rainy family camping trip.
Then we wrap it all up,
and take it home,
where I have my hot bubble bath.

Now, I am seeing tents everywhere I go.
Neon green domes under motorway bridges.
Bright yellow triangles in local parks.
Red wind-torn arches resting on cold concrete.

I imagine lying in my small tent,
where my hair rubs against the small squeezed space.
Like a birthday balloon building static,
my feet rubbing the zipped entrance,
my head touching the opposite end.
I try to imagine a whole home in this small space.

I think of the tents that have been ripped and torn,
by angry men with batons in hand.
Smoke and canisters,
stinging eyes and full force.
Horse hooves and shields.

And I imagine someone like me.
Missing their tent,
nowhere to go after the event,
with nothing but stars to look up at.

Family Reunion

Meet me by the shallow waters that glow fluorescent.
If I could, my body I would lay down as a shipwreck,
offer a home to the clams and anemones.
I would kiss craters of ultraviolet back into the bleached white,
Bandage tendril-like algae over the grey tinge,
sprinkle striking pigments over the breakages.

Meet me by the shallow waters that glow fluorescent.
Let's wipe a rainbow of colours across the polyps.
Take it all in, the hues of reds, oranges, and pinks.
I will be waiting there, where marine life is thriving,
next to this living breathing body of symbiosis,
teeming with urchins and sponges of cyan.
Meet me by the shallow waters that glow fluorescent.

The grown-ups stubborn in their arguments
make the distance stretch between us over years.
But there was a time, when we made holiday memories,
of diving, floating and wave watching on sandy beaches.
So, meet me by the shallow waters that glow fluorescent,
let us heal the distance that time has made.

Where Am I?

I am your instant travel guide,
take me in, and I will transport you
across lost places and ancient times.
There is nowhere I cannot take you.

Share me with your sleepy family
at the end of a long arduous day.
Or bundled in galactic duvet covers,
under the glare of a bright torch.

Spend time with me in the spring blossoms,
or let's lie on picnic blankets on seafronts.
Let's go to cafes and spend hours sipping a tea,
or we can cosy up next to a roaring log fire.

Write about the unravelling magic of me,
treat me kindly and without judgement.
Be careful with my delicate spine,
turn softly to my open and trusting nature.

Listen to me out loud,
or whisper to me quietly.
Share me with classrooms,
or swap me with friends.

Whether far or near, once we have met,
I am sure I will always stay in your imagination.

Answer: In a book

Where Are You *From* From?

In ancient times your name was spoken here,
beneath the thickets and shadow of trees.

Its echo can be heard in the river of this valley.
A gentle lull, that longs for you here.

Once, centuries before, when you were a giant,
you stepped over waters to reach the crest of mountains.

The word of you is still a magic that ties people and place across time.
These footsteps of yours have been here since the birth of this land.

The legends of you are alive here. You are one and the same,
this place of forest and stone and wise rush of river.

This gentle ground under your feet
will not turn away the curiosity of you,

because deep down in the bones of here,
is the living breathing heartbeat of you.

Little Man of the House

Little man of the house,
I worry about you.
Even though I know
there are many 'little men of the house'.
Your father before you was,
my brother is,
and I'm sure my father was once too.
I worry what love looks like to you.
Quite possibly it is all hurt,
and partings,
and the grasping
at strands of what once was.
Little man of the house,
does my love suffocate you?
Your chores have doubled up.
The hoovering is your job.
The recycling too.

So, I have started to sit you in gardens.
We push our hands into the earth,
sow seeds,
wait for sun and rain,
wait for tomorrow.
We are re-learning that love is
a beautiful responsibility,
and it is patience,
and all our dreams,
in that small first sprouting.
All green and fragile
against the morning light.

Glossary

Azaan	call to prayer
Chaat	a yoghurt dip
Djinn	spirits (both good and bad)
Dua	a personal prayer to Allah
Dupatta	headscarf
Eid	a day of celebration for Muslims
Fajr	dawn prayer
Gulab jamum	Indian sweetmeat
Hadith	the sayings of the prophet
Halal	permitted
Hammam	Moroccan Bath house
Harsha	a crumbly North African dessert

Henna	patterned red dye to decorate the hands with
Hijab	a hair covering
Iftar	the opening of the fast
'Inna Lillahi wa inna ilayhi raji'un'	'Indeed we belong to Allah, to Allah we return'
Jabal al Nar	Mountain of Fire
Jhumkeh earrings	traditional umbrella shaped earrings
Jummah Prayers	Friday Prayers
Kaftan	traditional dress worn by women
Keema and mattar	mince meat with peas
Khari Sharif	a shrine in the area of Mirpur
'Kitnah sonah tainu rab neh banya Dil kar dekh ta rahoun'	'How beautiful the Creator has made you; I wish I could look upon you forever.'

Kunaffe	A cheesy Middle Eastern dessert
Maghrib	evening prayer
Masala	spice
'Meh Punjabi bolniya'	'I speak Punjabi'
Pakul	traditional flat cap
Qawwali ghazals	Pakistani poetic music
Ramadan	the Islamic month of fasting from dawn to dusk
Sehri	the close of the fast
Shalwar kameez	a traditional shirt and trouser suit
Sherwani	the coat of men's trouser suit
'SubhanAllah'	'All praise is due to Allah'
Suhur	breakfast at dawn
Zakat	charity

Acknowledgements

First and foremost, I would like to thank Allah, Who is the best of planners. This collection could not have been written, had it not been for the journey my life has taken me on.

I am eternally grateful to the many people who have offered me help, guidance and motivation to become a writer. To Joseph Coelho, for his patience, generosity and for pushing me that little further – and to Roy Johnson my editor, for his patience and belief in this collection, and for holding my hand through this journey. To Glenn Carmichael and the Poetry Society for giving me opportunities to work with young people and learn from them. To Dream Arts, the schools in Tower Hamlets and all the young people who have worked with me over the years and given me inspiration to write. To Apples and Snakes for their continuous support in developing my work. And finally, to Arts Council England who supported me in writing this collection.

About the Author

Shagufta K. Iqbal is a dyslexic writer who grew up in Bristol and now lives in London, with her husband, her children and step-children, her cats and tea cups. There are many places she has called a home, but this is by far her favourite one. She writes about place and belonging, because family and community are important to her, whatever that family may look like. She is passionate about sharing poems about all the different kinds of love we hold, and how we build these relationships, whether it is with Allah, romantic relationships, familial, community, or love of nature, and she always writes about food. Her children's stories include *Bibi and Rumi* and *The Spelling Bee*, she has contributed to *Spin!*, and *Slam!* poetry anthologies, and is writing a children's picture book called *There Are Cats in the Mosque*.

Everything In-between is her first full children's collection. She loves baking, and climbing mountains, (but not at the same time, because taking an oven up a mountain would just be silly!)

About this Collection

We love publishing poetry at Troika; it's been a pleasure and a privilege to work with the poets on our small list. The aim of Troika Firsts is to bring together a first full collection of poetry by a poet who may have had individual poems published in anthologies or elsewhere, but who has not yet published a cohesive collection of their work that showcases their individual and unique voice and style. We're delighted and thrilled to be publishing Shagufta's first collection.

troika

The home of great children's books

Troika is a small independent children's book publisher. We're based in the UK.

Follow us on social media

@TroikaBooks

@troikabooks

@TroikaBooks